PUFFIN BOOKS

EUROPE UP AND AWAY!
Eurofacts and Eurofun

There is a tunnel being built underneath the English Channel that is bringing the British Isles closer to the rest of Europe. This book will show you around all the different countries in Western Europe from Iceland to the British Isles to Greece. You'll meet all sorts of children who live there, from Klara who lives in Sweden, to Pablo who lives near the Costa Brava in Spain. You'll probably want to know all kinds of different things about them, like what do these children do for fun? What do they eat? How do they dress? Are they very different from you? How can you get a penfriend and what should you write? What is the EC and what is so important about 1992? Is there really a midnight sun, and what is a haggis?

This invaluable introduction to Europe answers these questions and more. With masses of interesting facts, illustrations, maps and quizzes, this is definitely a fun way to find out all about Western Europe.

Sue Finnie is expertly qualified to write about Europe. She has lived in England, Scotland, France and Italy and speaks four languages. She has travelled extensively in Europe and has also been a language teacher and an editor of foreign language magazines, writing many articles and teaching packs. She is married, has two young sons and lives in Perthshire, Scotland.

Sue Finnie
EUROPE
UP AND AWAY!
Eurofacts and Eurofun

Illustrated by
Keith Brumpton

PUFFIN BOOKS

With thanks to the Press Office of the Commission of the European
Communities for their advice on pages 90 and 91.

PUFFIN BOOKS
Published by the Penguin Group
27 Wrights Lane, London W8 5TZ, England
Viking Penguin Inc., 40 West 23rd Street, New York, New York 10010,
USA
Penguin Books Australia Ltd, Ringwood, Victoria, Australia
Penguin Books Canada Ltd, 2801 John Street, Markham, Ontario, Canada
L3R 1B4
Penguin Books (NZ) Ltd, 182–190 Wairau Road, Auckland 10, New
Zealand

Penguin Books Ltd, Registered Offices: Harmondsworth, Middlesex, England

First published 1990
10 9 8 7 6 5 4 3 2 1

Typeset by Rowland Phototypesetting Ltd, Bury St Edmunds, Suffolk
Made and printed in Great Britain by Cox and Wyman Ltd, Reading, Berks.

CONTENTS

WHAT IS EUROPE?

Andrew lives in Glasgow in Scotland.

Greta lives in Bergen in Norway.

Jean-Christophe lives in Geneva in Switzerland.

Maria-Manuela lives in Lisbon in Portugal.

Nikos lives in Thessaloniki in Greece.

These girls and boys all live in different countries.
They speak different languages.
Each of them has a very different way of life.
But they have something in common.
Can you guess what it is?
They are all EUROPEAN; they all live in Europe.
This book is all about EUROPE.

Where Do You Live?

Look at this letter. The envelope gives us a lot of information.

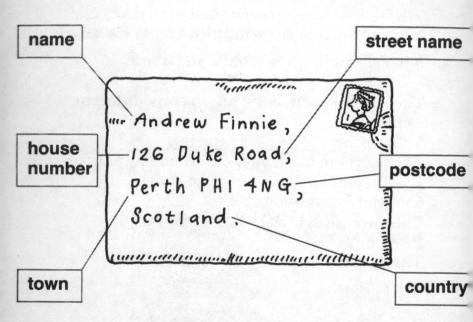

name

street name

house number

postcode

Andrew Finnie,
126 Duke Road,
Perth PH1 4NG,
Scotland.

town

country

● Your home is in a street, which is in or near a village or town. Your town is in a country.

Do you know the name of your street? Your town? Your country?

The world is very big. It is made up of lots of different countries.

Our World

This is our world. This is what it would look like if you were in a spaceship high above the Earth.

● Two thirds of the Earth's surface is covered in water – oceans and seas, lakes and rivers. Only about one third of the Earth's surface is land.

Continents

The land areas of the world are divided into seven continents. Asia is the largest continent. Australasia is the smallest continent.
● Each of these continents is made up of a number of countries. Do you know which continent your country is part of?

The world is round, like a ball. This is what it would look like if it were opened out flat.

North America

Europe

Asia

Africa

South America

Australasia

Antarctica

The Continent of Europe

Europe is quite a small continent. It is made up of more than thirty countries. These countries are some of the richest in the world. They have efficient farms and industries.

● Unlike some of the bigger continents, the land and the weather are not the same in different parts of Europe. Would you like to live in the icy Arctic regions of the far north? Or would you prefer the hot, dry, sunny countries in the south, near the Mediterranean Sea?

If you visit another European country, you will notice other differences too. In each country the people have their own way of life. They speak different languages and use different money.

Different people have different ideas on how to run their countries. Europe is divided into two parts: Eastern Europe and Western Europe. This book is about the countries and people of Western Europe.

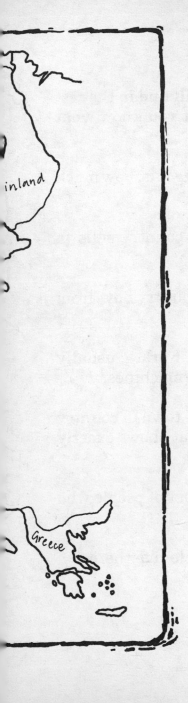

inland

Greece

The Countries of Western Europe

Andorra
Austria
Belgium
Denmark
England
Finland
France
Greece
Iceland
Ireland
Italy
Liechtenstein
Luxembourg
Malta
Monaco
Netherlands
Norway
Portugal
San Marino
Scotland
Spain
Sweden
Switzerland
Vatican City
Wales
West Germany

WORDCHECK

Here are some words you will find in the rest of the book. Check now that you know what they mean.

AREA (of a country): how big it is, how much land it covers.

EXPORT: something one country sells to another country.

IMPORT: something one country buys from another country.

INDUSTRY: type of work, usually involving lots of people and machines.

MAP: diagram of a place (a town, a country or even the whole world) that shows exactly where things are.

POPULATION: the number of people who live in a place.

UNINHABITED: no people live there.

NORTHERN EUROPE

Can you see the sun at midnight? Yes! There are places north of the Arctic Circle where the sun does not set at all on at least one day of the year. It is light all day and all night. Sometimes this part of the world is called 'the Land of the Midnight Sun'.

● In northern Europe it is light and bright in summer, but summer is short. Winter is long and dark and cold.

Hundreds of years ago, the Viking people left the mountains, lakes and forests of northern Europe to explore the world in boats called longships.

Three of the northern countries of Europe — Denmark, Sweden and Norway — are sometimes known as Scandinavia.

Iceland
ISLAND

Database
People: Icelanders
Official language: Icelandic
Population: 247,024
Area: 103,000 square km
Capital city: Reykjavik
Money: Nýkronur

Do you know which European country has the most volcanoes? Iceland. Iceland is a large island just south of the Arctic Circle.

Most of the country is made up of mountains. Over a hundred of these mountains are really volcanoes. As the centre of the island is so mountainous, nearly all the towns and villages are near the coast.

What is a Volcano?
A mountain with hot liquid rock in the middle. When a volcano erupts, the liquid rock is thrown high into the air.

● Winter in Iceland is very cold. Icelanders make warm pullovers, hats, socks and gloves from the soft wool of long-haired sheep.

A lot of people use hot water to heat their homes. The water comes from geysers. A geyser is a natural spring which throws out boiling water and steam. The largest geyser throws out 200 litres of boiling water every second!

In winter a lot of the roads are blocked by snow. It can be difficult to get to school. Children who live on farms have to stay with a friend or relative in the city from Monday to Friday. They can only go home at weekends.

Icelandic children don't start school until they are seven.

Finland
SUOMI

Database
People: Finns
Official languages: Finnish and Swedish
Population: 4,901,000
Area: 338,145 square km
Capital city: Helsinki
Money: Markka

In Finland you are never far from a lake. There are about 60 thousand of them. The Finnish people call their country Suomi. In their language that means 'lakeland'. There are lots of forests too. They cover almost the whole land. Wood from the trees has many uses. Some is used to build houses and much of it is pulped and made into paper. There is not much good land for farming and not many big towns.

● The sauna was invented in Finland and people like to have them in their homes.

What is a Sauna?
A special room full of steam. When you sit in it, the heat makes you sweat. This cleans your skin. Afterwards you take a cold shower or bath.

Winter in Finland is long and cold, but it can be fun. Finnish children learn to ski when they are very young. Schools give all the children a ski-ing holiday every winter.

Finns love sport. Many of the world's top skiers, long-distance runners and javelin throwers come from Finland.

Norway
NORGE

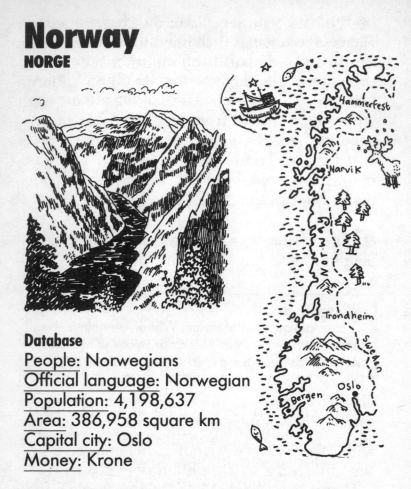

Database
People: Norwegians
Official language: Norwegian
Population: 4,198,637
Area: 386,958 square km
Capital city: Oslo
Money: Krone

The north of Norway is wild, mountainous countryside. You can meet more bears and lynx there than people! The most northerly town in the world is in Norway. It is called Hammerfest. There are not many towns in this part of the country. Most Norwegians live near the capital city, Oslo.

● Norway is a long, narrow country with a jagged coastline. It is hard to build roads or railways because of the mountains.

Norway is famous for its fjords. Fjords cut inland from the sea between the high mountains making a spectacular landscape.

What is a Fjord?
A very long, narrow inlet of the sea with steep, mountainous sides. Long ago enormous blocks of ice carved out steep valleys which were filled by the sea when the ice melted.

With such a long coastline, it is not surprising that the sea is important. Norway has a great shipping fleet. Lots of people work as fishermen. They go out on small boats to fish for cod. You may have eaten some Norwegian fish. Most of the fish caught in Norway is exported to other countries.

This funny little man is a troll. Trolls are said to come from Norway. You can read about them in fairy stories but they never really existed!

A troll

Sweden
SVERIGE

Database
People: Swedes
Official language: Swedish
Population: 8,400,000
Area: 450,000 square km
Capital city: Stockholm
Money: Krona

Midsummer

How would you like to wear a crown of lighted candles? This is Klara. She is nine years old and she lives in Stockholm. She is dressed as Saint Lucia for a very important day. It is 13 December, the Festival of Lights. Swedish people look forward to this day to brighten up the long, dark winter.

Read what Klara has to say about some other holidays she enjoys:

24 December
Christmas Eve

'We have a special supper of herring, ham and rice porridge. Then Father Christmas comes with presents, or we gather round the Christmas tree to hand out gifts.'

Easter

'We dress up as witches and go from house to house collecting sweets or money.'

30 April
Valborg

'At nightfall we light a bonfire and sing songs. This is to celebrate the return of the sun and the warm weather.'

Last day of school

'Summer holidays start at the beginning of June. On the last day of the school year we decorate the classroom with flowers. We all wear our best clothes.'

Midsummer

'We decorate a maypole with flowers and leaves. We dance round it. We can stay up all night.'

Denmark
DANMARK

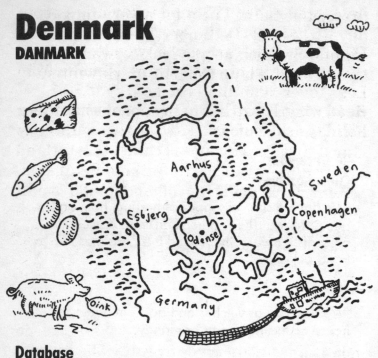

Database

People: Danes
Official language: Danish
Population: 5,175,000
Area: 43,069 square km (not including Greenland)
Capital city: Copenhagen
Money: Danish krone

Did you know that you may have a Danish toy in your home? Lego plastic building bricks! The word Lego comes from two Danish words *leg godt* meaning 'play well'. The Dane, Godfried Kurt Christiansen, invented Lego in 1958 and today it is a popular toy all over the world. If you go to Denmark you can see a wonderful Lego theme park where everything is made from Lego (over 30 million bricks!).

● Denmark is the smallest of the northern European countries. Part of the country is joined to Germany and is called the Jutland Peninsula. As well as the Jutland Peninsula, Denmark is made up of about 500 small islands. Most of these islands are close together. But one large island that is part of the Kingdom of Denmark is many miles away, near the North Pole. This island is Greenland, said to be the home of Father Christmas.

Denmark is a flat country; there are no mountains and hardly any hills. The highest point is only 173 metres above sea-level. Most of the land is farmland. A lot of bacon, butter, cheese and eggs are produced and sold to other countries. Pork is Denmark's main export. More than 10 million Danish pigs are reared for bacon production each year. Fishing for cod, plaice and herring is very important too.

Do you know the story of the Ugly Duckling who grew up to be a swan? That fairytale was written over a hundred years ago by a Dane – Hans Christian Andersen.

NORTHERN EUROPE QUIZ

How much do you remember about the countries of northern Europe?

Give yourself 3 points for a correct guess after 1 clue. 2 points for a correct guess after 2 clues. 1 point for a correct guess after 3 clues.

Which country am I?
1. A lot of my people use hot water from geysers to heat their homes.
2. I have more volcanoes than any other European country.
3. I am a large island just south of the Arctic Circle.

Which country am I?
1. My main export is pork.
2. Part of me is joined to Germany.
3. The inventor of Lego was born here.

Which country am I?
1. I am said to be the home of the trolls.
2. I am famous for my fjords.
3. My capital city is Oslo.

Answers on page 94.

If you scored:
7–9 points: Top marks. Well done!
4–6 points: Not bad.
0–3 points: Not very good. Read pages 15–25 again!

THE BRITISH ISLES

The British Isles are two large islands (Great Britain and Ireland) and many smaller islands. They are part of north-western Europe. The United Kingdom or Great Britain consists of four small countries: England, Wales, Scotland and Northern Ireland. The south of Ireland, called the Republic of Ireland, or Eire, is independent of the United Kingdom. Britain is small but it has played a large part in the history of the world.

> Britain is one of the most crowded places in the world.
>
> In England there are 355 people for every square kilometre.
>
> In the USA there are only 25 people for every square kilometre.
>
> And in Australia there are only 2!

England

Database
People: English
Official language: English
Population: 46,362,836
Area: 130,439 square km
Capital city: London
Money: Pound

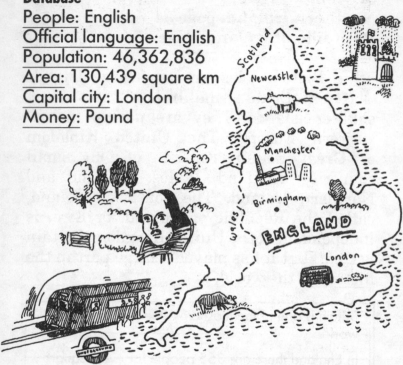

If you visit London, the Underground is a good way to travel round the busy city. London was the first city in the world to have an underground railway. There are lots of places to see:

Buckingham Palace – the home of the Queen
Big Ben and the Houses of Parliament

The Tower of London and Tower Bridge
Nelson's Column (and the pigeons!) in Trafalgar Square
Saint Paul's Cathedral

● If you are hungry, try some traditional English food. Have you tried these?

	YES	NO
Fish and chips		
Bangers and mash		
Steak and kidney pie		
Jellied eels		
Roast beef and Yorkshire pudding		
Shepherd's pie		

There are lots of different restaurants too, started by people originally from other countries who have settled in Britain. Italian, Indian and Chinese food are all popular.

Cricket is the national game, but rugby and
football are popular too.

The English countryside is pleasant but
four out of every five people live and work in
a town. The English love their gardens and
parks and there is plenty of rain to make the
grass nice and green.

The patron saint of England is Saint George. You
may know the story about Saint George killing a
dangerous dragon. But did you know that Saint
George was not English. He was probably born in
Turkey!

Wales
CYMRU

Database
People: Welsh
Official languages: Welsh and English
Population: 2,792,000
Area: 20,768 square km
Capital city: Cardiff
Money: Pound

Wales is smaller than England or Scotland. It is a land of mountains, coal-mines and music. Two out of every ten people speak the Welsh language. All road signs are written in Welsh as well as English.

● In 1969 Queen Elizabeth II gave her son Charles the title of Prince of Wales at a ceremony at Caernarfon Castle.

On Saint David's Day, 1 March, Welsh people wear a daffodil in their lapel. The daffodil is a symbol of Wales.

Scotland

Database
People: Scots
Official language: English
Population: 5,116,000
Area: 77,167 square km
Capital city: Edinburgh
Money: Pound

Britain's highest mountain, Ben Nevis (1,343 metres), is in Scotland. Parts of the country are mountainous and wild. There are many beautiful lakes, called lochs. One loch – Loch Ness – is famous because a monster is said to live in it. Quite a few people claim to have seen the Loch Ness Monster and even to have photos of it, but scientists don't believe in it.

● This is traditional Scottish costume. Most men wear a kilt on special occasions only these days. You can hear the bagpipes being played at traditional gatherings like the Highland Games. These games are a good chance to see some unusual sports like hammer-throwing and tossing the caber.

Since the discovery of natural gas and oil fields in the North Sea near Scotland, it has become the centre of the British oil industry.

The national dish is haggis. This is made from chopped meat, oatmeal and spices.

Northern Ireland
ULSTER

Database
People: Irish
Official language: English
Population: 1,562,200
Area: 14,122 square km
Capital city: Belfast
Money: Pound

Ireland has a long and violent history of struggles against England. Northern Ireland is part of Britain but the Republic of Ireland became an independent country in 1921.

Republic of Ireland

EIRE

Database

People: Irish

Official languages: Gaelic and English

Population: 3,537,195

Area: 70,283 square km

Capital city: Dublin

Money: Punt

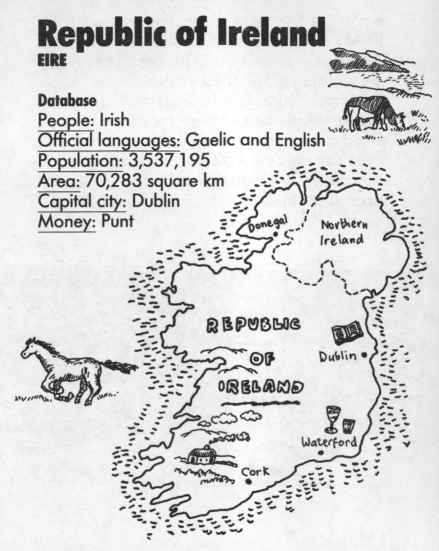

Ireland is sometimes called the Emerald Isle because of its green fields. The fields are a good home for the cows who produce a lot of milk, butter and cheese.

● Part of the land is covered by peat bogs. This is an area of wet ground in which dead leaves and plants rot. The peat that forms can be dug up and used as fuel.

Do you like horses? Irish horses are famous. Some of the best racehorses in the world come from Ireland.

On the west coast of Ireland you see lots of cottages like this. The roof is thatched with straw and the walls are whitewashed.

SPORT IN BRITAIN QUIZ

These sports are all popular in Britain. Can you guess what they are?

Answers on page 94.

CENTRAL EUROPE

In the middle of Western Europe are the two largest European countries: France and West Germany. France is the largest in area and West Germany has the largest population.

France
FRANCE

Database
People: French
Official language: French
Population: 55,751,000
Area: 551,000 square km
Capital city: Paris
Money: Franc

France is the largest country in Western Europe. It is twice as big as Britain, but it is still only one-fifteenth of the size of the USA.

39

● France is right in the middle of Europe. It has borders with six other countries, and England is only a few kilometres away across the English Channel.

Concorde – the World's Fastest Airliner!
The supersonic Concorde was built by French and British companies working together. It went into service in 1976 and carries 130 passengers at 2,100 kilometres an hour.

French people like their food and drink. There are unusual dishes like snails and frogs' legs, though not everybody eats those. But everyone eats bread with every meal. The long French stick is the most popular type. And there are hundreds of different cheeses.

Grapes are grown in many parts of France and most are made into wine. France produces one third of all the world's wine.

The Tour de France
The world's leading cycle race. Each year it has a new route (4,800 kilometres long) all round the country.

The French Open
One of the world's top four tennis tournaments.

The Le Mans 24-hour Race
Sports cars race all day and night on a special track round the town of Le Mans.

The Prix de l'Arc de Triomphe
The Longchamps course near Paris is where this world famous horse-race is run.

Andorra

Database
People: Andorrans
Official language: Catalan
Population: 32,700
Area: 453 square km
Capital city: Andorra la Vella
Money: French franc, Spanish peseta

Andorra is a tiny country high up in the Pyrenees mountains, on the border between France and Spain. The people work on farms or look after the tourists. Tourists come to ski in the winter.

Monaco

The Casino

Database
People: Monegasques
Official language: French
Population: 25,000
Area: 467 acres
Capital city: Monte Carlo
Money: French franc

This tiny country is in France, by the Mediterranean Sea. It is ruled by a prince, the head of the Grimaldi family. The main town, Monte Carlo, is famous for its casino, its annual car rally and racing Grand Prix.

West Germany
BUNDESREPUBLIK DEUTSCHLAND

Database

People: Germans

Official language: German

Population: 61,392,000

Area: 248,708 square km

Capital city: Bonn

Money: Mark

Do you know the story of the Pied Piper of Hamelin? If you go to Hamelin in Germany, you can see the Pied Piper and hear his magic flute. Every Sunday morning there is an open-air play in which the traditional story is acted out.

Karl-Heinz is German. He goes to school in Hamburg. He starts at 8 o'clock in the morning and finishes at 1 o'clock. In the afternoon there is no school, but he has to do 2 hours' homework.

● Today Germany is the greatest industrial power and the richest country in Europe. Engineering is the most important industry.

The first motorway in Europe was German. It was built in 1935 between Bonn and Cologne. Cars go very fast on the motorway. There is no speed limit on German motorways. On Sundays no trucks are allowed to travel, so the roads are quiet.

THE LOW COUNTRIES

Belgium: page 48
The Netherlands: page 50
Luxembourg: page 52

There are three 'low' countries: Belgium, the Netherlands and Luxembourg. They are flat, low-lying countries near the North Sea. There are lots of canals linking them to the sea and with other European countries. In recent times these countries have worked closely together.

Belgium
BELGIQUE/BELGIË

Database
People: Belgians
Official languages: French and Dutch
Population: 9,941,000
Area: 30,513 square km
Capital city: Brussels
Money: Belgian franc

If you like chocolate, you should visit Belgium. Belgian chocolates are world famous. There are shops selling nothing but chocolate – about 60 different types. They cost a lot of money because they are often handmade. But they taste delicious!

● Belgium is also famous for lace-making. Different towns have different designs for the lace they make.

Belgium is divided between the Flemish-speaking people and the French-speaking people. Things like street signs have to be written in both languages so that everyone can understand them. Sometimes names look quite different in the two languages:

The Belgian capital, Brussels, is sometimes called the capital of Europe. That is because the European Community (the EC) has its headquarters there.

Just outside Brussels is Waterloo. There was a famous battle at Waterloo in which the Duke of Wellington beat the French Emperor Napoleon. Today a huge statue of a lion marks the scene of the battle.

The cartoon character Tintin is Belgian. He first appeared in a Belgian comic more than 60 years ago!

THE NETHERLANDS
(also called Holland)
NEDERLAND

Database
People: Dutch
Official language: Dutch
Population: 14,717,000
Area: 41,863 square km
Capital city: Amsterdam
Money: Guilder

Holland is a *very* low-lying country. Nearly half the land is below sea-level. The Dutch have always had to spend a lot of time and

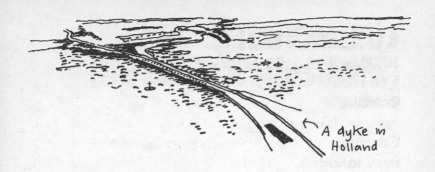

A dyke in Holland

money building sea-walls (dykes and dams) to stop their land being flooded.

● The city of Amsterdam is a criss-cross of canals. A boat trip is a good way to see the city. There are more than a thousand bridges to cross if you stay on land.

You see lots of bicycles in the Netherlands. 1½ million people have a bike. There are special cycle tracks everywhere. As there are no hills it's not hard work!

You see lots of windmills too. And in the spring there are millions of brightly coloured tulips.

Dutch people used to wear wooden shoes called clogs.

Saskia lives in Rotterdam. She says: 'Rotterdam is the largest city in the Netherlands. It is one of the most important ports in the world. I like to watch the big ships come and go.'

Luxembourg
LUXEMBOURG/LUXEMBURG

Database
People: Luxembourgers
Official languages: French and German
Population: 372,100
Area: 2,586 square km
Capital city: Luxembourg-Ville
Money: Luxembourg franc

Luxembourg is ruled by a Grand Duke, so it is known as a Grand Duchy. It is a small country between Belgium, France and West Germany. It has big iron and steel works and good farmland.

● Radio Luxemburg is an international radio station. It plays pop music 23 hours a day.

The European Court of Justice is in Luxembourg.

MOUNTAIN COUNTRIES

The Alps are a range of mountains in the south of Europe. They stretch from the French/Italian border across Switzerland, Germany and Austria to Yugoslavia. The highest peaks are covered with snow all year round. Mountain-climbing and ski-ing are popular sports. Some mountains are so high that you can ski above the level of the clouds!

Switzerland
SUISSE/DIE SCHWEIZ/SVIZZERA

Database
People: Swiss
Official languages: French, German and Italian
Population: 6,485,000
Area: 41,293 square km
Capital city: Bern
Money: Swiss franc

In Switzerland there are a lot of houses called chalets. They are made of wood. The roof slopes down steeply to help the snow slide off.

● Cuckoo clocks look a bit like Swiss chalets. The Swiss are famous clockmakers. A lot of cuckoo clocks come from Switzerland.

Swiss cows wear bells round their necks. This helps the farmer to find them if they are lost on the mountainside. He listens for the jingling of the bell.

This is an Alpine horn. Long horns like this were used to call the cows home at the end of the day. They make a loud noise.

Austria
ÖSTERREICH

Czechoslovakia

West Germany

River Danube

• Salzburg

Vienna

Innsbruck

Switzerland

AUSTRIA

Italy

Yugoslavia

Database
People: Austrians
Official language: German
Population: 7,575,700
Area: 83,849 square km
Capital city: Vienna
Money: Schilling

Austria has no coastline. It is completely surrounded by other countries. But there are a lot of lakes, and the River Danube runs through the country. The highest waterfall in Europe is in Austria. It is called the Krimml Waterfall.

● This is the Austrian national costume. Men and boys wear leather shorts and braces and a hat with a feather in. Women and girls wear gathered skirts and blouses with puffed sleeves.

Do you know how to yodel? Yodelling is an unusual type of singing. It was made famous by Austrians from the Tyrol region singing in the echoing mountains.

Many world-famous musicians were Austrian, including the following:

Strauss

Bruckner

Mozart

Liechtenstein
LIECHTENSTEIN

Database
People: Liechtensteiners
Official language: German
Population: 26,500
Area: 160 square km
Capital city: Vaduz
Money: Swiss franc

Liechtenstein is so small that it does not have its own language or money. You could walk the length of the country in a few hours. There are only 42 policemen in the whole country. Luckily there is not much crime!

● Liechtenstein is well known to stamp collectors. New stamps are issued every 3 months.

WHAT IS IT?
Can you remember what these are?
Which country would you find them in?

Answers on page 94.

MEDITERRANEAN COUNTRIES

The Mediterranean is a sea surrounded by the countries of southern Europe and North Africa. These countries have hot, dry summers and mild winters. Tourists come from the northern countries to enjoy beach holidays in the sunshine.

● But sometimes it can get a bit too hot! People put blinds or shutters on their windows to keep out the bright sunlight. This keeps their homes nice and cool. The hottest part of the day is between midday and 4 o'clock in the afternoon. In Mediterranean countries it is too hot to work then. Shops and offices close. People go home to rest or sleep. This is called a 'siesta'.

Spain
ESPAÑA

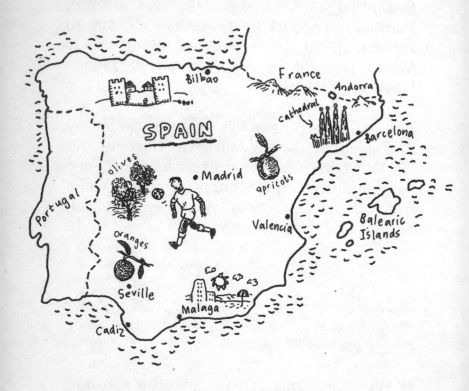

Database
People: Spanish
Official language: Spanish
Population: 38,400,000
Area: 504,788 square km (including the Canary Islands)
Capital city: Madrid
Money: Peseta

Spain is a great place for a holiday with its sun, sea, beaches, good food and wine. This is why Spain gets so many visitors. But there is another side to Spain. After Switzerland, Spain is the most mountainous country in Europe. The highest range of mountains is called the Sierra Nevada, which means 'snowy mountains'.

● Pablo is nine years old. He lives in a little village near the Costa Brava. He says:

'Costa Brava means "wild coast". It's called that because it is so rocky. In summer we love to go to the beach to swim and play on the rocks, but it gets crowded with all the tourists.

'We eat lunch late, usually between 2 and 3 in the afternoon. Dinner is at 9 p.m. My favourite food is paella. That is rice, chicken and seafood mixed together. On hot days we often have a cold soup called gazpacho.

'My father runs the village shop. In Spain shops usually stay open until 8 o'clock in the evening. They shut between 1.30 and 4.30 for lunch and a siesta.'

The flamenco is a special dance from Andalusia in the south of Spain. Dancers dance to guitars and castanets and the people clap their hands and tap their feet.

Spain produces more olive oil than any other country in the world. Olive trees don't need much water. They grow well on the dry hillsides.

Everyone eats oranges in Spain and they are an important export. Special oranges are grown near the town of Seville. They have a bitter taste and make good marmalade.

Pears, peaches, apricots and cherries are also grown. A lot of the fruit goes to factories where it is put into cans.

Spanish Islands

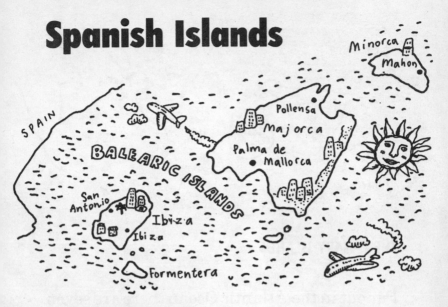

THE BALEARIC ISLANDS

The Balearics are a group of islands off the east coast of Spain. They used to be quiet and peaceful. There were not many visitors because it took a whole day to reach them by boat from Barcelona. But now jet planes mean tourists can reach the islands easily. Thousands of tourists choose these islands for a holiday.

● Majorca is the largest island and the most popular. The south and east coasts are busy places with hundreds of hotels. But you can still find peaceful places on the rest of the island, particularly away from the seaside towns.

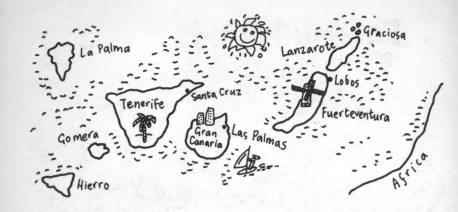

THE CANARY ISLANDS

Far out in the Atlantic Ocean there are seven small islands which belong to Spain. They are much nearer to Africa than to Spain.

● As you might expect, the weather is hot. It hardly ever rains, except in the mountains. The Canary Islands are popular for holidays all year round. It is hot even in winter.

What colour is sand? Yellow? Brown? White? Some beaches on these islands have *black* sand! It is made from volcanic lava broken up by the sea.

> The Canary Islands gave their name to the yellow bird, the canary.

Portugal
PORTUGAL

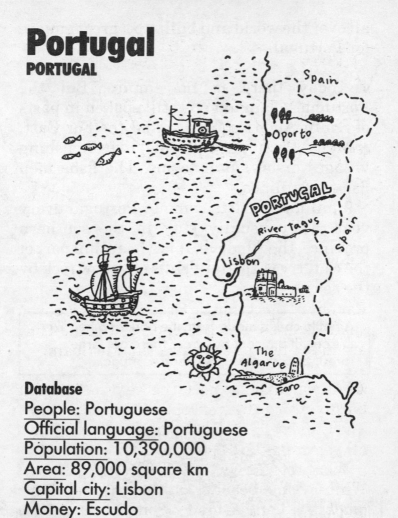

Database
People: Portuguese
Official language: Portuguese
Population: 10,390,000
Area: 89,000 square km
Capital city: Lisbon
Money: Escudo

Today Portugal is a small, poor country, but hundreds of years ago it was an important world power. Great explorers like Magellan, Vasco da Gama and Prince Henry the Navigator were Portuguese. They travelled all over the world and built up a great empire for Portugal.

● Today there is no empire. But the Portuguese language is still spoken in parts of South America, Africa and the Far East.

Many Portuguese people live in fishing villages or on small farms. The fishermen fish for sardines.

9 million tourists come to Portugal every year. They usually stay in the southern province, the Algarve. It is a beautiful part of the country with giant cliffs of yellow rock by the sea.

A bottle cork is made from the bark of a tree like this one. It is a cork oak tree. There are large forests of cork oaks in southern Portugal.

Bark of the Cork Oak

The Cork Oak

Leaf of the cork oak

Italy
ITALIA

Milan

Venice

Florence

Pisa

San Marino

ITALY

Rome & Vatican City

Naples

Sardinia

Cagliari

Palermo

Sicily

Database
People: Italians
Official language: Italian
Population: 57,000,000
Area: 301,225 square km
Capital city: Rome
Money: Lira

Italians love spaghetti. The Italian word *spago* means string. Can you see why spaghetti is a good name?

● Spaghetti is made from hard wheat, grown in the Po Valley, and water (and sometimes eggs). To eat it like a true Italian, twirl it round your fork. Don't cut it – it's unlucky! Spaghetti is just one type of pasta. There are nearly a hundred different types. They are all kinds of shapes.

Italians make good pizzas and ice-cream too.

This is Julius Caesar. He was a great emperor in Ancient Rome. His soldiers rode in chariots and had lots of battles. But they were also clever builders. The Romans built roads, bridges and aqueducts in many European countries.

Some people think the map of Italy looks like a boot. It is a long narrow country. The Appenine mountains run down the middle of the country. The north of Italy is richer than the south. All the big factories and good farmland are in the north.

Italy has many beautiful, historic cities. Perhaps the most unusual is Venice. Venice is built on little islands. There are no roads. People travel by small boats instead of cars and buses.

Italian Islands

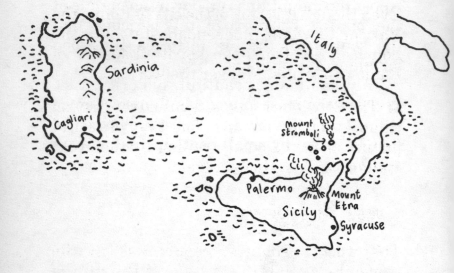

There are more than 70 islands off the coast of mainland Italy.

● The largest is Sicily. If you were a strong swimmer you could swim from the toe of Italy to Sicily. It is only 3.2 kilometres. Sicily is the home of Europe's largest volcano, Mount Etna.

Some of the smallest islands are uninhabited. Others, like Gorgona, are used as prisons for convicts.

Many of the islands – Sardinia, Capri, Elba and Ischia – are pleasant holiday spots. In Roman times, Ischia was especially popular . . . for its healthy mud baths!

The Vatican City

Even though it is part of the city of Rome, the Vatican City is an independent state. It is the home of the Pope, the spiritual leader of Roman Catholics all over the world.

● The Pope's own chapel is called the Sistine Chapel. It is famous for the beautiful pictures painted on the ceiling by the great Italian painter Michelangelo.

San Marino

The world's smallest republic is in the Appenine mountains in Italy. When all the tiny states of Italy decided to join together over a hundred years ago, San Marino chose not to join. Today San Marino is still an independent state.

● San Marino is famous for its beautiful postage stamps.

Malta

Database
People: Maltese
Official languages: English and Maltese
Population: 341,179
Area: 316 square km
Capital city: Valletta
Money: Maltese lira

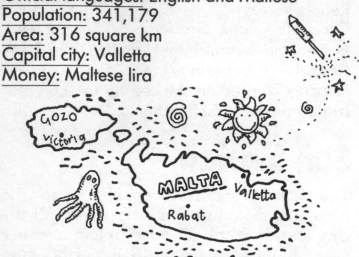

Do you like fireworks? Maltese people do. They have lots of festivals with fireworks to light up the night sky.

● There is never any snow or frost in Malta. It's a warm sunny island. There is not much rain, so the people have to be careful not to waste water, particularly in summer. Malta is rather flat with no lakes or rivers.

Maltese fishermen catch lots of interesting fish. Stew made from cuttlefish and octopus is popular.

Greece
ΕΛΛΑΔΑ

Database
People: Greeks
Official language: Greek
Population: 9,665,000
Area: 131,957 square km
Capital city: Athens
Money: Drachma

People visit Greece for the beaches, the museums and the archaeological sites. The Ancient Greeks were brilliant people. Even the clever Romans studied their art and ideas.

● The Greek language has its own alphabet of symbols.

The Olympic Games started in Greece. They started as a religious festival to honour the Greek God Zeus. That was nearly 3 thousand years ago! In those days women were not allowed to take part, or even to watch. Foreigners were not allowed either, just Greeks. The men competed naked. The prize for the winners was an olive branch.

Today things are quite different. The first modern-style Olympic Games were held in Athens in 1896. The Games are held every four years. They are the most important international sporting competition. Millions of people throughout the world watch the Olympic Games on television. Perhaps you have seen them.

From Greece we get:
lemons   grapes   tobacco   olives

Greek Islands

There are hundreds of little islands dotted around mainland Greece. Most are covered with mountains or hills. The people earn a living from fishing or from looking after tourists.

● The largest Greek island is Crete. The Palace of Knossos on Crete is one of the oldest buildings in the world. It was built about 4 thousand years ago!

Archæologists have discovered marble statues, jewellery, weapons, tools and pottery on these islands which are thousands of years old. They help us to understand how people used to live there many years ago.

What is an Archaeologist?
A person who finds and studies buildings and objects made by people who lived hundreds and thousands of years ago.

HOLIDAY POSTCARDS QUIZ

Which countries do you think these postcards have been sent from?

Answers on page 94.

GETTING TO KNOW OTHER EUROPEANS

How To Say 'Hallo'

We know that the people of Europe speak different languages. But did you know that some languages sound quite alike? These are languages that come from the same 'family'.

● Here's how to say 'hallo' in six European languages. Which languages do you think belong to the same family as French? Which languages do you think belong to the same family as German? *Answers on page 94.*

FRENCH	*Bonjour*
GERMAN	*Guten Tag*
ITALIAN	*Buon giorno*
SPANISH	*Buenos dias*
DUTCH	*Goed dag*
SWEDISH	*God dag*

Make a 'Europe' Scrapbook

You probably see a lot of European things every day. Perhaps you eat spaghetti that comes from Italy or oranges that come from Spain. Your butter may come from Denmark or Ireland. You might be surprised by how many European things you see.

● Why not start a European scrapbook? Here's what to do:

1. Write the name of a European country at the top of each page in your scrapbook.

2. Stick in labels of food from that country.

3. Ask your friends and family to save stamps and postcards from European countries for you to stick in.

4. Cut out pictures from old newspapers, magazines and travel brochures.

5. Draw pictures. Try copying some of those in this book if you like.

Penfriends

Bjorn lives in Sweden. He has a friend he has never met, who is called Steven. Steven lives in England. Steven and Bjorn are penfriends. They write letters to each other.

● Having a penfriend is a good way to find out about another country. You write and tell your friend about yourself, your family and so on. And you can ask questions about his or her way of life.

Bjorn speaks Swedish at home. He is learning English at school. His mother helps him to read Steven's letter and to write back in English.

If you want a penfriend, you can write to: International Youth Service, P.O. Box 125, 20101 Turku, Finland.

Collecting Stamps

This is the Penny Black stamp. It is the most famous stamp in the world. The Penny Black was the world's first stick-on postage stamp. It was invented in Britain by Sir Rowland Hill.

● Lots of people collect stamps. They keep them in an album. Some stamps can be worth a fortune.

WHY COLLECT STAMPS?
Stamps are colourful. They can tell you about the country they come from. Each stamp design can tell you something if you look at it carefully.

● Stamp-collecting is easy. Most people get letters with stamps on. Start your own stamp collection. Ask your family and friends to save their stamps for you. If you get two stamps the same, swap with a friend.

> Most countries put their name on their stamps. Britain is the only country in the world that does not. A British stamp just has the Queen's (or King's) head on it and the value.

Car-spotting

You can tell which country a car comes from if you look for a small sticker on the back of it. Usually the sticker shows the first letter of the country's name.

● Can you say which European countries these cars are from?

Some are not so easy. Would you have guessed these?

This car comes from Spain.

 This is from Switzerland.

This is from Austria.

See if you can spot any European cars in your town, or when you visit another town or country.

In most European countries cars drive on the right-hand side of the road. The steering wheel is on the left-hand side of the car. In Britain cars drive on the left-hand side of the road. They have their steering wheel on the right.

Cars are made in many European countries. In most countries you can buy a car made in your own country or a car imported from another country.

Working Together

Is the world getting smaller? You may have heard people say that it is. It isn't really. But today the world often seems smaller than it is because it is so easy to travel to other countries.

● Modern inventions like planes, telephones and TV satellites bring people in different countries closer together. It is important for people in different countries to live and work together. This is why a tunnel is being built under the Channel between England and France, bringing the British Isles closer to the rest of Europe.

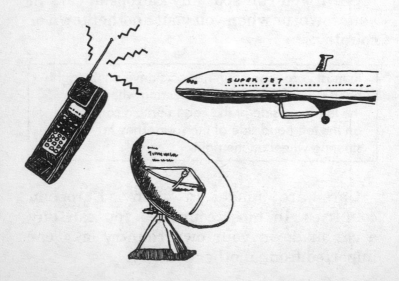

THE EUROPEAN COMMUNITY

Twelve of the countries in Europe have joined together. They call themselves the European Community. They want to work together and help each other. They don't want their countries to be cut off from each other. They want to be one large community. This will help them to be an important world power.

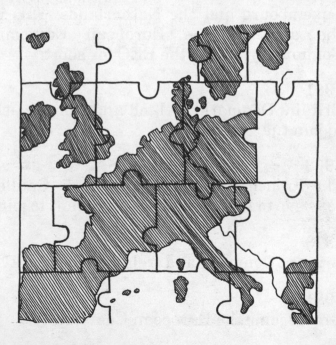

87

How the European Community Started

1945
The end of World War Two. The people of Europe begin to think about how they can live together in peace instead of fighting.

1957
Six European countries sign an agreement to help each other. The agreement is called the Treaty of Rome. The six countries are Belgium, France, West Germany, Italy, Luxembourg and the Netherlands. This is the start of the European Economic Community, called the EEC for short.

1961
Britain, Denmark, Ireland and Norway ask to join the EEC.

1963
The French President, General de Gaulle, says 'no' to those countries who want to join.

1973
Britain, Denmark and Ireland join the EEC.

1981
Greece joins the European Community.

1986
Spain and Portugal join too.
There are now twelve countries in the EC.

1992
Single European Market.
Special laws make it even easier to work in
and trade with other countries in the EC.

Common Policies

> **What is a Policy?**
> A plan a group intends to carry out.

The twelve countries of the European
Community work together by all having the
same policies. These include:

The Common Agricultural Policy to improve
farming.

A social policy to improve people's living and
working conditions.

A regional policy to make rich regions help
the poorer regions.

A transport policy to allow people and goods
to move freely between countries.

How it Works

The European Community has four institutions to help it carry out its work.

1. The Council of Ministers

This group is made up of one minister from each member country. It has regular meetings and makes important policy decisions, like those on page 89.

2. The European Commission

This group is responsible for thinking up the EC's plans and then seeing that they are carried out. The larger member countries (West Germany, Spain, France, Italy and Britain) send two commissioners each, and the smaller countries (Belgium, Denmark, Greece, Ireland, Luxembourg, the Netherlands and Portugal) each send one. So there are 17 commissioners altogether.

3. The European Court of Justice

The court is in Luxembourg. 13 judges hear cases involving Community law. All member countries have agreed to accept the court's judgements.

4. The European Parliament

The Parliament has its meetings in

Strasbourg, in France. There are 518 members of this Parliament. They are called MEPs (Members of the European Parliament). Large countries have more MEPs than small countries. The job of the Parliament is to discuss the policies and to say whether it thinks they will be good for the European Community or not.

Citizens of Europe

If you travel to another country, you need a passport. European countries used to have their own passports. Nowadays, European Community countries all have the same passport – a European passport.

● A European passport shows you belong not just to your own country. It shows that you belong to Europe.

MAP QUIZ
Name the Country

Look at the map on page 93. The names of the countries are missing. Work out which name goes with each number. Try to do it without looking back! The first one has been done for you.

. . 16 . Austria
. . . . . Belgium
. . . . . Denmark
. . . . . England
. . . . . Finland
. . . . . France
. . . . . Greece
. . . . . Iceland
. . . . . Ireland
. . . . . Italy
. . . . . Liechtenstein
. . . . . Luxembourg
. . . . . Malta
. . . . . Netherlands
. . . . . Norway
. . . . . Portugal
. . . . . Scotland
. . . . . Spain
. . . . . Sweden
. . . . . Switzerland
. . . . . Wales
. . . . . West Germany

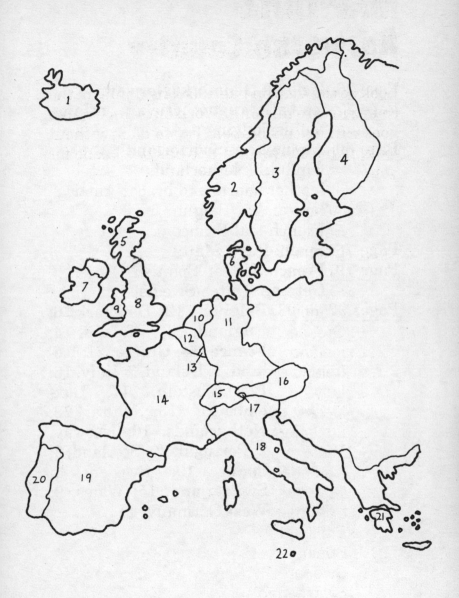

Answers on page 94.

Answers

Page 26: Iceland; Denmark; Norway
Page 37: football; rugby; cricket; fishing; tennis; jogging
Page 60: Alpine horn/Switzerland
windmill/Netherlands
leather shorts and braces/Austria
lace-maker/Belgium
French loaf/France
Page 78: Spain; Italy; Malta
Page 79: French: Italian/Spanish
German: Dutch/Swedish
Pages 92 & 93: Belgium, 12; Denmark, 6; England, 8; Finland, 4; France, 14; Greece, 21; Iceland, 1; Ireland, 7; Italy, 18; Liechtenstein, 17; Luxembourg, 13; Malta, 22; Netherlands, 10; Norway, 2; Portugal, 20; Scotland, 5; Spain, 19; Sweden, 3; Switzerland, 15; Wales, 9; West Germany, 11.

INDEX